LITTLE EXPLORER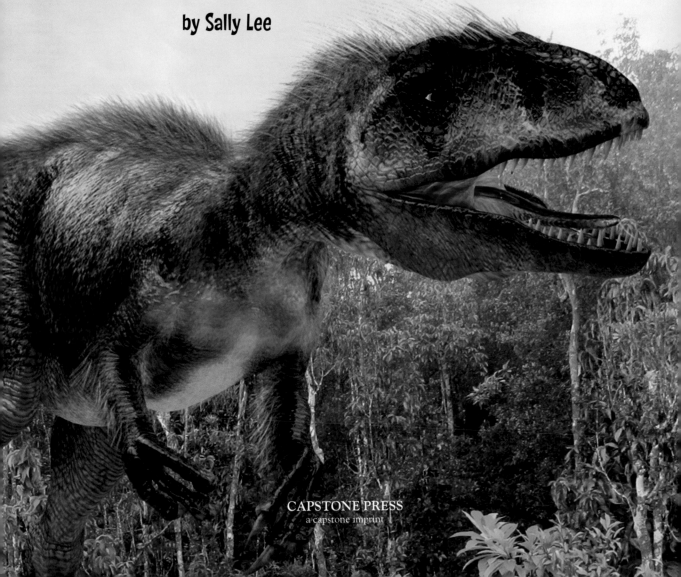

ALLOSAURUS

by Sally Lee

CAPSTONE PRESS
a capstone imprint

Little Explorer is published by Capstone Press,
1710 Roe Crest Drive, North Mankato, Minnesota 56003
www.capstonepub.com

Library of Congress Cataloging-in-Publication Data
Lee, Sally, 1943– author.
Allosaurus / by Sally Lee.
pages cm.—(Smithsonian Little explorer. Little paleontologist)
Summary: "Introduces young readers to Allosaurus, including
physical characteristics, habitat, behavior, diet, and fossil
discovery"—Provided by publisher.
Audience: Ages 4–7
Audience: K to grade 3.
Includes index.
ISBN 978-1-4914-2127-7 (library binding)
ISBN 978-1-4914-2374-5 (paperback)
ISBN 978-1-4914-2378-3 (paper over board)
ISBN 978-1-4914-2382-0 (eBook PDF)
1. Allosaurus—Juvenile literature. 2. Paleontology—Jurassic—
Juvenile literature. 3. Dinosaurs—Juvenile literature. I. Title.
QE862.S3L437 2015
567.912—dc23   2014021796

Editorial Credits
Michelle Hasselius, editor; Heidi Thompson,
designer; Wanda Winch, media researcher;
Tori Abraham, production specialist

Our very special thanks to Mike Brett-Surman, PhD, Museum
Specialist for Fossil Dinosaurs, Reptiles, Amphibians, and Fish at the
National Museum of Natural History, Smithsonian Institution, for his
curatorial review. Capstone would also like to thank Kealy Wilson,
Product Development Manager, and the following at Smithsonian
Enterprises: Ellen Nanney, Licensing Manager; Brigid Ferraro,
Vice President, Education and Consumer Products; Carol LeBlanc,
Senior Vice President, Education and Consumer Products.

Image Credits
Corbis: Michael S. Yamashita, 8; Davide Bonadonna, 28–29;
iStockphoto: David Parsons, 20 (bottom left); Jon Hughes, cover, 1,
2–3, 5, 6–7, 9, 12–13 (all), 14, 16–17, 17 (top left), 18–25; Newscom:
Photoshot/El Snow, 11; Sauriermuseum Aathal: Urs Möckli, 26–27
(all); Science Source: Francois Gohier, 23 (bottom right), Publiphoto,
30–31; Shutterstock: BACO, 4 (bus), Catmando, 17 (top right),
Denis Pepin, 19 (br), dkvektor, 17 (bl), Fidel, 10 (bird), Kostyantyn
Ivanyshen, 7 (right), reallyround, 5 (br), Steffen Foerster, 5 (bl),
Steve Bower, 15, T4W4, 4 (folder), Viktorya170377, 4 (bl), 17 (br)

Printed in Canada.
092014   008478FRS15

TABLE OF CONTENTS

name: Allosaurus

how to say it: al-oh-SAW-rus

when it lived: late Jurassic Period, Mesozoic Era

what it ate: meat

size: 30 to 40 feet
(9.1 to 12 meters) long
7 feet (2.1 m) tall from
the ground to its hips
weighed 2 to 3 tons
(1.8 to 2.7 metric tons)

Allosaurus was one of the deadliest dinosaurs during the late Jurassic Period. This fearsome predator made its home in what is now North America.

Thanks to FOSSILS

A fossil is evidence of life from the past. Fossils of things like bones, teeth, and tracks found in the earth have taught us everything we know about dinosaurs.

MEET ALLOSAURUS

short horns above eyes

large head

bony ridges on nose

knifelike teeth

large claws on hands and feet

Allosaurus belonged
to a group of dinosaurs
called theropods. These
dinosaurs ate meat and
walked on two legs.

stiff tail

padded feet

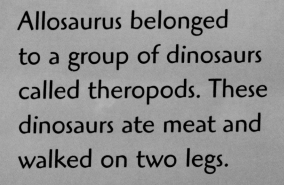

Tyrannosaurus rex

Allosaurus looked like a
small Tyrannosaurus rex. But
Tyrannosaurus rex lived millions
of years after Allosaurus.

HOOKED CLAWS

Allosaurus's arms were short but strong. Each hand had three fingers with curved claws. The dinosaur used them like meat hooks to dig into prey.

Allosaurus claws grew up to 6 inches (15 centimeters) long.

fossilized claws of an Allosaurus

Like other huge dinosaurs, Allosaurus had padding on its feet. The padding helped protect the bottom of the dinosaur's feet when it walked.

Allosaurus had three large, clawed toes. It also had a small fourth toe on the side of each foot.

DIFFERENT BONES

Allosaurus means "different lizard." The dinosaur got its name because of holes found in its backbone. Scientists once thought Allosaurus was the only dinosaur that had these holes. Today we know that all theropods had holes in their backbones.

Allosaurus skeleton at the Dinosaur National Monument in Utah

bluethroat

Allosaurus had a wishbone in its chest. Birds also have wishbones.

Allosaurus had a second set of ribs called gastralia. Gastralia grew inside Allosaurus's belly.

KNIFELIKE TEETH

Scientists used computers to study Allosaurus's jaws. They learned the dinosaur's bite wasn't like other meat eaters'.

"Allosaurus had a relatively weak bite ... and probably wasn't able to splinter thick bone."

—paleontologist Emily Rayfield

Its bite may have been weak, but its teeth were deadly. Allosaurus used its sharp teeth like knives to slash and tear at its prey. Its teeth curved backward. This made it harder for prey to escape once inside the dinosaur's mouth.

Allosaurus's knifelike teeth were 2 to 4 inches (5 to 10 cm) long.

HOLEY HEAD

Unlike other meat eaters, Allosaurus had two short horns above its eyes. It also had long, bony ridges on each side of its nose. The horns and ridges may have protected its eyes. They also could have helped attract a mate.

Allosaurus's head was strong. It could take hard hits during fierce attacks on other dinosaurs.

Allosaurus had several large, open spaces in its skull. These spaces made the dinosaur's skull lighter.

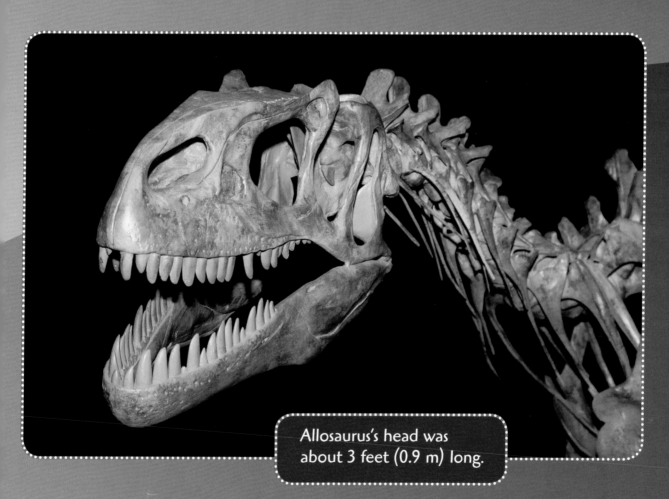

Allosaurus's head was about 3 feet (0.9 m) long.

JURASSIC HOME

Allosaurus lived where the states of Utah, Colorado, Montana, and Wyoming are today. The dinosaur made its home on flat land near streams and rivers.

The Jurassic Period lasted from 200 million to 145 million years ago.

DINOSAUR ERA

TRIASSIC	JURASSIC	CRETACEOUS
252	200	145	66	present

millions of years ago

Other Jurassic Animals

Apatosaurus

Camptosaurus

Diplodocus

Stegosaurus

These areas were warm during the late Jurassic Period. They had rainy seasons followed by long dry periods. The warm weather helped conifers, cycads, and ferns grow.

DEADLY HUNTER

Allosaurus was a carnivore. That means it ate meat. Allosauruses may have joined together to attack larger plant-eating dinosaurs.

Scientists do not believe Allosaurus lived in herds. Some Allosaurus fossils have been found together. It is likely they were just feeding on the same animal when they died.

Allosaurus probably hunted alone for small prey. The dinosaur was also a scavenger. It ate what was left over from another dinosaur's kill.

Coyotes often hunt in groups to attack larger animals.

OUT TO KILL

Allosaurus trackways in Colorado

Trackways are sets of prehistoric footprints found in rocks. They give scientists clues about how dinosaurs moved and lived. Allosaurus usually walked on its toes. Scientists know this by studying the trackways the dinosaur left behind.

Allosaurus was a quick killer.
It dashed toward its prey with its
mouth open. Its strong upper
jaw slammed down like an ax.

Bite marks on fossils show
Allosauruses also attacked
one another. They probably
fought over food and mates.

ON THE MOVE

Allosaurus used its large tail to keep its body balanced when it walked or ran.

The dinosaur had large, powerful legs to outrun its prey. Allosaurus probably ran about 20 miles (32 kilometers) per hour.

Scientists dig for Allosaurus bones in the Morrison Formation

Some scientists think it was dangerous for Allosaurus to run. If the dinosaur fell, Allosaurus's arms were too short to break its fall. Allosaurus fossils show many broken bones due to falls.

EGGS AND BABIES

All dinosaurs hatched from eggs.
Scientists think the female Allosaurus
buried its eggs under piles of plants,
like a crocodile does. The heat from
the rotting plants kept the eggs warm.

Scientists studied the fossil of a 10-year-old Allosaurus female. They can guess a dinosaur's age by counting the growth rings in its bones.

BIG AL AND BIG AL 2

The first Allosaurus bones were found in Colorado in 1877. But the most exciting discoveries happened more than 100 years later.

Big Al

Paleontologist Kirby Siber and his team found a nearly complete Allosaurus skeleton in Wyoming in 1991. They named it Big Al.

Big Al 2

People learned about Big Al from the TV special *The Ballad of Big Al*. It showed what the dinosaur's life might have been like.

Five years later Siber's team found an even bigger Allosaurus skeleton. They named it Big Al 2.

PREDATOR TRAP

Utah's Cleveland-Lloyd Quarry is a huge bone bed. More than 12,000 dinosaur fossils have been found there.

That amazing number includes parts of more than 40 Allosaurus skeletons.

More predators than prey have been found at the quarry. Some scientists think that's because it was a predator trap. In a predator trap, plant-eating dinosaurs got stuck in mud.

Predators tried to eat the stuck dinosaurs, but they also got caught in the sticky goo.

Allosaurus is the most commonly found dinosaur fossil in Utah. It is Utah's official state fossil.

GLOSSARY

bone bed—a single layer of rock that contains a large number of fossils

conifer—a tree with cones and narrow leaves called needles

cycad—a plant shaped like a tall pineapple with palmlike leaves

fern—a plant with finely divided leaves called fronds

fossil—evidence of life from the geologic past

gastralia—belly ribs that are not connected to the backbone

herd—a large group of animals that lives or moves together

meat hook—a sharp metal hook used to hang meat

Mesozoic Era—the age of the dinosaurs, which includes the Triassic, Jurassic, and Cretaceous periods; when the first birds, mammals, and flowers appeared

paleontologist—a scientist who studies fossils

predator—an animal that hunts other animals for food

prey—an animal that is hunted by another animal for food

quarry—a place where large amounts of stone are dug out of the ground

ribs—curved bones around your chest

scavenger—an animal that feeds on animals that are already dead

skull—the set of bones in the head; the skull protects the brain, eyes, and ears

theropod—a meat-eating dinosaur that moved on two legs

wishbone—a bone shaped like a "V" between the neck and chest; birds have wishbones

CRITICAL THINKING USING THE COMMON CORE

Allosaurus was one of the most deadly predators during the late Jurassic Period. What is a predator? Name an animal that is a predator today. (Craft and Structure)

Read the fact on page 23. Why do scientists think it was dangerous for Allosaurus to run? (Key Ideas and Details)

Turn to page 28. Explain in your own words how Allosaurus could have died in the Cleveland-Lloyd Quarry. (Integration of Knowledge and Ideas)

READ MORE

O'Hearn, Michael. *Allosaurus vs. Brachiosaurus: Might Against Height.* Dinosaur Wars. Capstone Press, 2010.

Raatma, Lucia. *Allosaurus.* 21st Century Junior Library: Dinosaurs. Ann Arbor, Mich.: Cherry Lake Pub., 2013.

Rockwood, Leigh. *Allosaurus.* Dinosaurs Ruled! New York: PowerKids Press, 2012.

INTERNET SITES

FactHound offers a safe, fun way to find Internet sites related to this book. All of the sites on FactHound have been researched by our staff.

Here's all you do:

Visit *www.facthound.com*

Type in this code: 9781491421277

Check out projects, games and lots more at
www.capstonekids.com

Super-cool stuff!

INDEX